CW00506385

I lived and was schooled in
educationalist and later studyir
career started in London, anc
Cornwall, where I led an Arts
of Art/Technology. I was also Art Advisor to Cornwall County
Council.

I have travelled extensively; cycling around Europe,
(5000+ miles in three months), worked on a Kibbutz in Israel,
and undertook the 'hippie trail' overland to Nepal, as well as
embarking on numerous South East Asian journeys.

I was previously married, fathering two children. After two
years separation, I bought a farm jointly with my subsequent
partner, and over fours years, created habitats for wildlife.
I then moved to Bath, alternating between there and Andalucia,
Spain. This was followed by a period of serial monogamy and
polyamory, as I explored tantra.

I bought a van, and lived in it on Dartmoor in Devon, for
a year, painting in a barn studio. Following a serious septicaemia
infection which hospitalised me, I moved into Bowden House
Community, Totnes. During the two years there, I learnt and
practised deep tissue, sensual and tantric massage.

Since arriving in Bristol four years ago, I have written
daily. I am inspired by Buddhist, Zen and Taoist philosophy
and practice. I continue to paint and have exhibited for over
25 years, and my work is in private collections throughout
the UK, California, Japan and Denmark. Currently I paint in
a studio in central Bristol and follow my other passions: playing
guitar, dancing to trance music, and table tennis!

For further information visit www.vincentrymer.co.uk.

BRISTOL SADHU

VINCENT RYMER

VOLUME ONE

SilverWood

Published in 2016 by SilverWood Books

SilverWood Books Ltd
14 Small Street, Bristol, BS1 1DE, United Kingdom
www.silverwoodbooks.co.uk

ISBN 978-1-78132-524-7 (paperback)

British Library Cataloguing in Publication Data
A CIP catalogue record for this book is available
from the British Library

Set in Sabon by SilverWood Books
Printed by Blissetts on responsibly sourced paper

Contents

Preface

I wish to share some of my journey in life with you. A journey entailing a complex navigation through a continuing 'rites of passage' and 'rites of passion'. I have taken innumerable sojourns into the tantric jungle matrix, we call the world.

My evolution has been immeasurably enriched by the illuministic immensity of, love and sex; arguably the two most potent energies on the planet. My revolution has been indelibly accelerated by the practice of vigilant presence; in living every breath-filled moment, whereby everything becomes possible and pleasurable...nurturing. I wish to thrive, to be in perpetual expansion, to realise my fertile-potentiality and creative-fecundity; and to share these visions and perceptions.

I invite you to enter through the portal of poetry and commune as spiritual-hedonistic sisters and brothers, lovers and live-ers! To embrace 'stillness and motion'; not dualistically or duel-istically; but from the vitalising perspectives of: immersion, connectedness, synchronicity, harmony, surrender and empowerment...and when awakened, to stay awake, even in your dream-enlightened sleep.

Vincent
January 2016

1 The Great Journey

I am a nomad, I wander throughout time.
Place to place, from face to face,
Human race, to human race.

I am a nomad, I wander throughout time,
Body to body, passions aroused,
Leaving history behind, leaving histories...Behind.

I am a nomad, I wander throughout time,
Treading unknowable pathways...intuit-a-lively,
Always meeting the unforeseen, and beyond the dream.

I am a nomad, I wander throughout time.
The movement is peace, the movement is my release,
Pausing just long enough, between moments...Moments.

I am a nomad, I wander throughout time,
And only restlessness...persists,
Meeting and parting, converging and resisting.

I am a nomad, I wander throughout time,
Following vibrations, inside, and from afar,
All is possible, surfing the waves, of my inner...radar.

I am a nomad, I wander throughout time,
Treading pathways into the void of nothingness,
And everything is something, becoming...becoming!

I am a nomad, I wander, and time passes…
Through me, wanting nothing, and everything…
And all I need is within, and…sing-ing.

I am a nomad, travelling as light as I breathe,
And breath, is the rhythm of the living,
All flowing in between…in-bet-ween!

I am a nomad…dancing…Dancing…
Dancing the eternal dance, between…
Motion and stillness…in love's infinite dream.

September 2015

2 The Birth of the Universe, Beyond, 'Big Bang', and Black Holes

No male or female copulation.
No matriarchy, patriarchy, oligarchy...hierarchy,
Just love, energy joyously exploding.
An ecstatic communion of intrinsic, existential pleasure
    manifesting,
Releasing supranovae luminosity...
Quasars and pulsars, electrons, shedding atomic energy
    throughout...
The deep, borderless vastness of space,
And splattering it with galactic starlit...spermatozoa,
An orgasmic pulsing that vitalised every particle with the breath
    of life.

A vibratory expanded breath that did not:
Separate,
Isolate,
Insulate, or
Violate.

The magnitude was, and is...incalculable,
Beyond the inanity of mathematical speculative...projection.
It exists, and within its fathomless, effulgent field...it gives,
And it gives...with a cosmic...open heart.

Our very emanation from this cosmic womb...
Continues to be an evolutionary miracle,
A miraculous, revolutionary, perpetuating...miracle.
A cosmic odyssey in time and timelessness, which,

Has no *de-fin-it-ive* boundaries; neither, chaotic or…formulaic,
It is beyond all, its ignitive coition…is beyond,
The captivity of cognition.
It is the breath of universal being…with its own volition.
It nourishes, it is generative and replenishing.
It has given form and substance, to the Earth,
As we know it…and continue to know it…
In its totality…all-enveloping, wholeness.

No words can really describe…can encapsulate…!

When you feel the pulse, the heartbeat of the universe,
Its vibration, reverberates; into, through and out of…
And love penetrates and bathes, all in a starlight illumination.
An omniscient, omnipotent, procreative…luminosity,
That impregnates, animates the entire cosmic ocean,
Giving its harmonious gift…to the music of equilibrium!

There is no:
Conductor,
Orchestrator, or
Arbitrator.
There are no border controls.
There is only the love that ensued from the first…
Explosive ejaculation.
A beatific, meglomomentary climax.

Love…begetting love…!
Begetting love,
And in that sublime, divine birth…Genesis.

And there is only non-dual homogeneity,
That scientific-religious misogyny cannot belie.

We must break free from the shadows of the
Deterministic;
Into the fluidity of spontaneous uncertainty!

The universe will only be subsumed,
When Genesis…becomes…genocide.
When its breath can no longer be sustained by love.

This universal womb is the home to all and everything,
Every species, known, and unspecified.
Every microcosm in the vastness of the macro-ocean.

Our love, consciousness, flows in this great current,
Wave after synchronistic wave…infinite and…indiscriminating.

There is only existence, beyond knowing…in the uterus of feeling,
An amorphous pulsation, resonating throughout the seamless
    sea of symbiotic galaxies.

And here I dwell enraptured with a transcendent, euphoric,
Sensation of sublimity and belonging…a oneness of being.

This oneness is not this, or that…or otherness.
It is the intimate immensity of love's embrace,
And I surrender to this, quintessential realisation,
And there is only…the self-less-self,
Immersed within the miraculous, fructifying, immutable…
Cosmic breath…
The source of life…
In the universal womb…of all…
Existence!

December 2014 and July 2015

Harmony of the Spheres 120 x 152cm

3 Into the Box (the coffin of consciousness and individuality)

Can you fit in?

Fit into the box; fit in from the outside in?

Can you fit in from the inside…without debilitating sublimation?

Can you conform, condone soporific and sacrificial filiation.

Will you authorise, the abusive sterility of chloroform
    consciousness.

Yes…so anaesthetise yourself; cauterise the wounded self,
    in conformity and entropy,

Completing the stunted cycle; an alienated, procrastinated,
    constipated…self.

Contort, distort, but fit in…fuck it, just fit in,

Belong, belong to the sleeping throng,

The consensual throng of human-inanity.

Just fit in, get inside the box,

Give way, give way; to belong, to belong…its intoxin-cating,

All shapes, all forms, all persuasions, and deliberations,

Just become an aberration to…yourself, corseted and cosseted,

Knowing you have negated yourself, to become incarcerated,

And truly, truly, LOST!

May 2014

4 Archaeology

I searched through the ruins of lost lives,
Excavated with bloodied fingers as memories evaporated into a
Translucent membrane of history.

Breaking through the encrusted skin, down below the epidermis,
Into the delicate heart fibres, down into the bowels, and
Into the soul body: of the dead, dying, and resurrected.
Sweeping aside the culturally deposited (bric-a-brac);
The intrepid accumulation of objects, and tired, emasculated
     objectives.
Fools' gold masquerading as visions,
Imposed by the politically correct and anal-retarded.

It is only in the darkened passages of the sub-terranean,
We see unblinded, the truth of each others' reality.
We feel beyond the frozen fabric of pretention and insipid
     convention,
Percolating in drip-feed propaganda designed:
To stifle, suffocate our pre-conceived freedoms,
Our floating dreams dredged, and forged meglomanically...
Into politicised, religious repressive alchemy.

Only...in the intuitive and primal excavations, do I discover
Who lies there...breathing in a purified air,
Found in dreaming!
Only...in the ruins of deconstruction, in buried telepathic
     temples do I find transition.
Below the lava embroiled surface, beyond the shrinking mask,
Beyond the inane, and delusional, do I find the truth.

In a reality of atavistic, knowing and feeling,
Beyond the pontifications of priests, preachers and teachers of
    personal treason.
Politicised proclamations and constipated posturing,
Beyond the polluted, decaying altruism of self-acclaimed
Sages, gurus and anchorites, secluded…internally contained,
Outside the secular, yet voicing a vernacular of,
Deceived wisdom and innocence.

Only…when the skin is pierced, peeled and shed, and the
Tongue tastes the marrow at the very core,
Do I find what is not here in this material world.
Lying obliquely in yesterday's debris our history portrayed in…
Warring and mystery.

Postulates, apostates, cleanse themselves in medicated waters,
Steeped in the mineral deposits of society's paranoia.
How many fears does it take, to infiltrate, the fear…of fear!

Fear that percolates, nourished by the misguided and blinded.
How the media relishes the power and carnage,
Cherishes the manipulation of disintegration,
Implicit and complicit in every headline banner, and
    sound-bite-ing!
The manner of which debilitates the vulnerable and gullible.

A pervasive sickness permeates and inhabits the unnurtured ego,
Wrenches the feeble-hearted into a blighted…crescendo.
Darkness descends and the light retreats into shadow.

Excavate: know your destiny is not un-consecrated fear…
    spoken…as fate.

Be passionate: a lack of conviction becomes an insuperable...
    affliction.
No clarity, leads to disparity, to disparity.

Do not let the cowardly, bury your sacred, your sanctity,
In the ruins of their profanity.
Excavate, liberate; cast off the shackles,
Cast off the burden...of doubt and indecision.
Cast-off!

An anchor must not become a noose...of the unconscious.
A fallen feather of a grey-lag-ged goose...adrift and lost.

Lost in the journey,

Do not lose yourself,

In the journey.

January 2014

5 Who The F.U.C.K is Alice?

I saw her fleetingly vanish through an aperture...wonderstruck!
No right, or wrong turning, just the fantasy of reality unfolding.

I beckoned her back, but it was her time...her time...to wander.
To roam, fleet footed, upon the mirrored path, to find her way
     home.
I thought I saw her smiling in that momentary turning glance,
But bedazzled by the sunlight, all was surreally askance.
It could have been any one of you, or all of you as one,
That had taken flight into that fanciful navel haven,
Under the watchful gaze of a whimsical white wizard,
Who tinkered in Tolkien tomfoolery...
And the allegorical art of the illusionary.

She ran through the long grass, strewn with perfumed poppies,
Purple spotted and dotted in garlands woven wild and golden,
Her skip-like run, became a dance that spun...
Her round and round...and roundddddddd!!!
Until the dream profound,
Became a fiction, right there upon the ground.

Stories sung and spun, mushrooming into rainbow realms,
As she hopped upon each starlit note, a cosmic, crazy-paving,
A constellated rave, into the hallucinogenic heart
Of the Milky Way's musical wave upon wavering;
As jingly-jangly, jabber-wacky gibberish prose arose,
A rhapsodic twittering of aubergenie magic transported Alice,
Who blew bubbled blossoms to the four winds of destiny's
     dreaming?

An enchantment that mesmerised this nomadic stargazer and
astral traveller,
Tending her Narnia garden, a prismatic paradise of paradoxical
creations,
Evoking the inner child...pristine!

Is nothing, just nothing? Or a seed of something...in the
imagination
And then everything is in the believing...in perpetual
incarnation.

A zero mind, is beyond the blindness of the mindless!!

Who the...

Fantasian,
Utopian,
Cosmo-gician,
Karmic-angel-astralician!

Is Alice?

Why...*Alice is in all of us*!

We just sleep too much to dream!

Rabbit...rabbit...rabbit

Tea anyone...?!

June 2014

Blue Portal 60 x 60cm

6 Enchanted Auras

The vastness of the past lies turbulently seething in the...
Rise and falling...of the tides...retrieving.

Moon cycles, song seeking, familiar reposts, resting...wist-fully,
In memories that mesmerise, the idolatry of reminiscences.
Attached by threads silken, broken but not forsaken.

The questions have ceased...answers lie submerged, in the...
Subconscious subterranean, and only solace remains.
And romance, reeks of wanting...desiring all of that...
That once stood, full and strong.

When the citadels have fallen, and the monuments of hope...
Have somehow been eclipsed.
The essence of what is, flows through the veins,
In a process of reforming,
Leaving pale, fleet, moving shadows...
That flits between moments of mute recognition,
And all is not abandoned between glimpses...
As the emotions are stirred in another's...reality.
Feelings roam free in unchartered territory.

On the prairie, where the grasses sway freely.
In the breezes of reflection, and light shines through...
The refractive bars of the orb's prism.

And I find you there...I find you there...
And the heart stirs, and tears fall freely in the sighs of my...
Sadness...

That churns the waters and a smile burns the skin of my
    knowing.
That lies in the cinders of the mind's parchments.

I was there, and you were here…and oneness prevailed…
In love,
And love knew no boundaries,
And all breathed in the beauty of our existence,
That persists, and enlists the memories lying deep,
In the vastness of time and space, interwoven in the…
The mind's meandering matrix,
Where echoes enter…

And the heart hears,
And the heart sees…
And the heart feels.

And yes, you are there…in here…
Here between the sheets…
The sheets of destinies creating…
In the rise and fall of…recalling.
Ghostly attachments ostracised in the mind's subconscious…
Cling to the umbilical;
And: I hear you.

I feel you.

I feel you.

I feel you,

In the clairvoyant stillness of the…

Memories…

Beating…

Eyes!!

August 2014

7 Crest of the Wave

Don't waste it, don't waste it...waste it!
Create it...vibrate, express, commune-icate,
Be it, breathe it, celebrate...and love it.

Be ready for the wave, ride it...glide it,
Find yourself...in it, with it...go...with it.
Immerse, converse, traverse...fly and swim.
Let the heart, mind and soul swim in the healing sea of seren-dip-ity.

This is the portal to your sanity.

This is the altar of your sanctity.

Know the only place is...

Know the only space is...

Know the only time is...

Know that the only thing you need to do...

Is to do it...Whatever that is...Do it!
Live it, be it, be it...don't waste the wave.
It may be the most significant...
You will ever be gifted.
This gift...is your gift.
Free it...Free it!!!!

September 2014

8 Bristol, Graffiti City

Walls, fences, defences; breached barriers…life in the city
   offences.
Keep outs, private, prohibited and lockouts.
Artists at twilight, ranting, chanting and planting,
Seeds for change, voicing rage and wonder, announcing a new
   golden age.
Art creating choices, for the disenfranchised reprobates…
Ostracised, patronised and revolutionised, a rupturing of the
   systemised and civilised.

And outlaw pranksy, has become an in-law at the Banksy,
And the street has lost the irreverent rancour of his activist,
   surreptitious feet.
He now a legend on 'red carpet'…celebrity beat.
A poignant revolutionary rebel – upbeat!

The iconic, ironic and menacingly moronic,
Daub and spray, and splatter the new chatter!
Visual tricksters and hipsters, mimics and mystics, vandals
   and…vampires,
Mingle and merge in dreamscapes, with the trite, brash and
   enlightened.

City nature: concrete, plastic, metal, stone and the architects'
   contrite; shielded, shielded from the blight.
Concrete jungles illumined by the street artists' light.
A manifesto to dazzle and frazzle, the new renaissance birthed…
   unearthed!
In the daubs, drips and droplets,

New age prophets proselytising populist images sprayed and
frayed…
Icons of the capitalists decayed.
Their ethics portrayed, and morals betrayed.

Blanketed walls replenished by the: heraldic hieroglyphic, and
calligraphic.
Tagging, specific and shambolic, pastiche and masquerade,
A playful angry bittersweet charade.
Exploding and unfolding, parodic; paradisal and anecdotal,
Stories interweaving; from the political, chimerical and cruelly
absurd,
An expanding city canvas warring and weeping,
Shadowed and sun seeking…
The inescapable inscapes seething and raving: a 'Las Vegas
Loathing'
Fears, graphic and super photo-reeling,
Camouflaged, under posters, torn, tattered and groaning,
moaning…
A miasmic megalomania: imprints, signatures, and endless
tagging.
Contemporary 'popness', explosive and corrosive peacock
displays,
Screaming…'Look at me, what do you see,'
Between the grey bleakness and twee.
What do you see amongst the city's debris?

Islands of the fantastical, diabolical, magical and maniacal,
Juxtaposed imagery, garnished and barbed, branded with the
bland, and the Blinded, the incoherent and the wise, jumbled
and crumpled,
In a sea of graffiti…in a sea of graffiti.

Anarchic, cannibalistic and ritualistic.
A destructive and creative simmering symbiosis,
Our lives germinating, fermenting and reformulating futures,
Dreamt and deceiving, breathing and breathless,
Treasured and impoverished, cherished and demolished.
Every surface, a mirror and a whirlpool of survival,
A dark hole devouring dreams and regurgitating fears,
Raising smiles, opening hearts; a vibrant cocktail,
A plethora of voices, idolised and incognito;
An alter ego…a screeching sax alto.

Hear me. Look at what I have done to this city,
And what this city has done to me!

I cry, and I sing, lament and I vent,
Celebrate and hate, desecrate and decorate,
Bosch, Grosz and Basqui-a-t.
All is street cred; and the 'reds' no longer hide their anger,
Under the beds of silent thunder…!

Lightning strikes across the city; the new pulse, voicing rage and
        wonder,
Beauty in disorder, mutating slogans and mantras…grandiose,
To awaken the sanitised slumber of the comatosed.

Bristol, a city of *vi-tal-ity.*

See, and hear me, feel me, the songs of my experience,
The innocence, violence and benevolence of my race,
Here, right now…in this new golden age!!

October 2014

9 Because You're Worth It…!

His hands caress your lustre, soft, pristine skin…trusting.

His fingers gently probe the delicate tissues…
And tenderness is all…within.

He fondles, slides and glides…over your sunbeam face,
Glazing your mouth, as your lips…suck his fingertips.
Your tongue curling delectably around his affectionate…
Sensitive hands!

He runs his fingers through your hair,
And all is glowing, flowing…over…and…into…you.

His unwashed hands carry the germ-infected grime,
Of the toilet; the loo, lavatory, urinal, piss-pot…excrete-eria.

Sacred and sanctified by the secreted,
Shit and pee that permeates all in the inner sanctuary.

He shares this all with you…
In love…in his oblivious exuberance,
In his toiletry extravagance,
All yours to relish…

Given freely…given freely…
To yours truly.
Because you're worth it!

June 2015

10 Building Site Demolition and Deconstructive Beauty?

Yesterday's ruins lie in temporary repose,
Transitional beauty breathes amidst the dismantled remains,
Dismembered fragments, relics of yesterday's buildings.
A deconstructive mausoleum,
An apocalyptic carcass, sprawled; it's skeleton,
Exposed amongst the un-curated excavations and
    transformations,
In a continual process of disintegration,
A systematic disembodiment!
A thoroughly emasculating dissection,
Creating a pitted skyline panorama,
Exposing: entrances, exits, portals, through, out and...

Into; interior – exterior conjunctions...and rupture.
And in crevices, hollows and asthmatic fissures,
Jewels incarnated, catch the light between dancing dust particles,
Colours of every hue and subtlety; surfaces textured, matt and
    shiny,
Shimmering and mirroring,
A sparkling alchemy, an artist's oasis.
The inert, animated, naked and uncensored...
Dangling, -nucleolus-like concrete blocks,
desiccated slabs,
Once a floor, a ceiling, a wall, a room, a bed...now dead!
Scarred surfaces; decorative and utilitarian, featuring yesterday's
    products:

Pipes, iron rods, plastic conduits and wires, just hanging...

Hanging synapses disconnected, ripped, slashed and
    pneumatically pulverised,
Hanging…suspended in space and timelessness,
A conglomeration of masticated musical notes; poignantly
    sonorous,
Melodic conduits forming the polyphonic bars of a new
    symphony.

Visual music…visual music.

Inspirational in its infinite juxtapositions, improvisational
    perambulations and spectral syncopations.

A new wonder-filled wasteland.
Resplendently disposable.
The building's heart, speared, intestines and vital organs…
Splayed, frayed, quartered and slaughtered,
A surgical cauterisation…revealing a magnificent corpse.
A Titian, a Rembrandt, a Decapitated De Kooning.

And I see nothing but beauty,
Beauty beyond the crudity…
The annihilated, obliterated remains…victuals,
Each exposed limb, fabric and fabrication arouses impulses,
Like an infection…manifesting.
Gigantic dinosaur-like machines, a contemporary Tyranno-
    saurus Rex…venting!
Its mechanical teeth and jaws: biting and tearing flesh from
    bone…
Sinews, fibres, flying viscera…

Carrion fodder for reclamatory vultures.

Demolition, the site of ironic, ephemeral beauty,
A dissonant rhapsody…erasure, erasure…Erasure.
Yet the mind's eyes, sees, sees…and feels,
In the lingering mind's eye's memories.
Paintings forming the legacy, embedded in re-creation,

An evocative requiem to impermanence!

October–December 2014

Demolition – No 2 51 x 41cm

11 Placebo Culture, Sedatives for the Sedentary

Take it, take it; internalise, fantasise, patronise…placate
    yourself.
Take it, take it; till you make it…happen…fake it!
Take it, take it; till you succumb to its…pregnant impotency.

Placebo culture; a culture of manufacture and fracture,
A culture designed by the vulture, to subvert, convert and…
    capture.
Placebo culture; miraculously lugubrious, fatuous and fabu-lust!

Take it, take it, till you make it; the benefits are in the…believing,
The meaning you imbue, the beliefs you attach to the meaning.
Take it, take it; it frees you from taking the responsibility of…
    changing,
It frees you from the truth of your…deceiving!

Take it, make it take you into healing and…idolatrous revealing?
The healing is in the believing, that what you are taking,
Relieves you from your feeling of…needing.
Kneading and wielding the truth of your entropic…catharsis,
And changing the truth of your feeling!

Know the truth, know the truth, of this feeling…!

April–May 2014

12 The Disasters of War

A night of daggers, phantoms in flight,
The heat of a fervent fire burns late into the embers of night.
The flame of flamenco, ablaze in festive, furtive shadows.

Starry skies…a black sun, a red moon is weeping blood.

Andalucía a history steeped in mystery; secrets catacombed.
In cellars deep, no mirrors adorn the dark interiors,
No sunlit windows, or windblown doors secrete.
Starry skies clouded by a red moon shrouded in a gold-gilted…
    guilt.

Endless cycles of treason, terrorism, barbarism, perpetuating
    betrayal,
The sins of violence, and violated victimhood enraged.
Voices silenced by hatred and fear…and the crippled…
Romanticism of…fascism!

Procured power, and the demonic corruption by the
Monarchists, ecclesiasts, Antichrists and parasites.
Dynasties and legacies persist through famine and…feast,
Famine and feast!

Across the un-dug graves and scattered remains;
Dancing sparks accompany the silence of the persecuted, the
    executed…
The brutally berated, unconsecrated…Unconsecrated.
The cries of the silent persist, echoes of the inquisition…
The slaughter of innocence…of innocence.

Volatile Andalucía, Iberian horns are sharpened to intolerance.
Agony and ecstasy, amalgamated under the eyes of God's...
    ungodly.
The symphonic sighs of souls deceased...continue to weep,
Tears of blood, sweep down in torrents from the peaks.
A macabre mosaic...red rivers to shores of sleepy waters...
Turquoise flowing to African desert glowing...sands.

Goya, his visions in derision, dream images, nightmares...
Insurrection,
No absolution,
Bleak motifs, a patriot's humanity, portrays the insanity,
An artist's ironic profanity...portraying insanity.

Blood stains the earth, red earth, a wounded soil soaked...
In the vitality of the unborn.
The trees harbour gallows...and branches spout limbs...not leaves.
Carrion feed greedily on the viscera and victuals,
Sun-shrivelled organs of the unreprieved,
Blowing in the breeze.

Andaluz, the light shines, decorating each dawn.
The flowers fragrant, disguise, but do not hide...
The stench of the dead.
Corpses, decomposing in a state...of frag-ment.
The butterflies, dancing here and there, as petals unfold...
To the click of heels and the plucked...guitar,

Plaintive ululations rise up, and the heart opens in joyfulness...
    and...
Juxtaposed grief.
In a staccato click of fingers from castanets, a disembowelled
    pain expressed,

A momentous, joyous, soulful expiration beneath a starlit
    constellation.

Granada, Alhambra, Andalucía, the Sierra Nevada.
Granada, a city of heart...artistry...
The rasp of silken songs delight...lacerated lamentations
    emancipated,
That echo through the cobbled streets and squares,
Of the Albacin and Sacramonte...in retreat!

Flamenco flames, rising in harmony, an iconic glory of...Iberian
    Spain,
A spring lamb's bleat.
A spring lamb's bleat.

The blood redness, sun-drenched madness,
An earth soaked in sadness.

The Matador's cloak entices...
The dancing bull; fire in its eyes, its nostrils flaring...glaring.

Her lips kissed the forehead; collapsing!
In the pain of a poisoned passion in despair...
The wolf languishes in its lair.
Her tousled hair...flows, as she twirls, twists and turns,
Her heels stamp onto a hardened, unyielding earth.
A bitter acerbic, salty blood spills down the skirt of her...
Pounding heart.

Heartbreak, inchoate, a culture present in its past.
A persistent, un-resistant exposed survival,
A magnificent and pitiful configuration...Church and...
    State!

A unison of flesh, bone, muscle and sinews clashing in;
Harmonious, rhythmic refrains; staccato, staccato, staccato,
Duende, duende, duende.
Inner life breathes, fertility, virility; a sombre felicity births...
A new revolution in chorus, and spits in undisguised disgust...
At the feet...
At the feet of oppressors, that brutalises the next generation of...
Converts and politicised perverts...in peace.

Flamenco burns into the scarred, embroidered, cauterised veins
of ancestors,
Where the blood runs deep and gypsy flowers,
Dazzle in the daze of a serried...summer, shimmering fiesta...
Siesta dreaming.

Ancestral juices oozing in the humid haze of a post...
Franco blaze...ablaze.

The majestic muscles bulge...
While its bull balls are castrate.

Matador, Paramour, love and death...love and death.
An immortalised marriage of Heaven and Hell united in...
Purity and a "*diaphanous*", sin...sin!

Blessings on the carnal and carnival...
Possessed in confessions, delirious in enigmatic celebratory
        processions.
The incarnate, an incandescent ascent...
Above the golden cupola, encapsulates, promises, a sublime...
        afterlife.
Divinity percolates in passivity, drifting in an enfeebled camphor
        of...belief.

Allah, Amen, Allah, Amen, Allah, Amen, Allah…Amen!
Olé, Olé, Olé…

Click, click, clickety-click, rat-a-tat-tat, castanets twitch…
Possession grips between the teeth…an apostate's grief.
A prostitute's belief…
In begetting, regrets submerged…
In the new morning light, obliterating the ablutions of a rancid
    sex night.

A black sun, a black sun and a red moon is weeping…weeping.

Suffering beasts, bellow in the sweltering, suppurating…heat,
That beats the brow in staccato repeats…repeats.

I hear the call of flamenco feet,
Flamenco cries of…laughter,
Tears nestled in the confines of a family campfire.

Almond blossom confetti, bedecks the earth in white,
In white.
In a white incubated…complete-ness.

Her smile: Madonna smile, incubus smile, harlot's smile,
    a mother's smile,
A lover's smile…a brother's smile, a sister's smile, another's smile,
It's time…it's time.
To feel the healing of a newborn breeze…
And the balm,
Of
Camomile.

August–September 2013

13 Intimate Palette

Satin skin, cerise pink lusciousness, body sultry moist.
How I love this word: moist, moisten, moistening…moistness.

A glistening pink skin, soft pastel pink inflamed;
Sex-tinted and awakened into vermillion heat…!

Eyes azure, dawn-blue-sky-sea tranquil turquoise…emerald
    and aquamarine,
Deepening into oil-black, dreamy opalescent devouring…An
    entranced glance.

An unconcealed nakedness, the layers burnt-umber away…in
    ardour,
Outer to inner opacity, to transparency; aurora green, iridescent
    tranquillity.

Lips, geisha-red, LUSH…sex-painted, rose-scarlet-crimson…
    sparkling,
Vampiric violet, musk, purple-haze…enticement!

The kiss, red to rosy pink, magenta-browns, copper, ochre,
White into black night.

Kissed, and blessed, lips suffused and tender,
Arousal…passionate…blood-red and…carnal.

Her pudenda flower-garden, a kaleidoscopic scented…
    aphrodisiac…haven.

Rainbow-bright, and jasmine beguiles under an indigo sky in...
    moonlight.

The pulse of her life inhaled, in-spired, radiant...spectral,
Multi-hued love...saturated intensity, ripe fruits...sated...
    insatiably.

Fragrant magnolia...waters...creamy...delicious and aromatic,
Milky-white...nourished in sunshine-yellow smiles of delight.

Orange-blossom love, resinous, honey-flowing...liquiscent,
Glowing...glistening amber-gold...a consummate
    crystallisation.

Her breath presence, gracious, opulent...an incandescent...
Candle light, illuminating each silvery...caress...Undress...ing.

Each golden gossamer touch; each aureole surrender,
Sylvan-warm moist...dark, cool, slate-grey salubrious...
    surrender.

Kisses perfumed pink, pellucid pink...impenetrably...ineffable,
Burning, majestically...through red heat, passion, tangerine
    tongues entwined...

In love and...forgetting,

Forgetting...in love.

June 2013 and September 2015

14 In the Zone

Ping..............................Pong

Delete,   Switch off.
Eradicate...   All...
And *everything*...   Other.
Outside the zone,   Surplus...Inside the head!

The arena,   The green table-top.
Edge to edge...   Perimeter.
Dissected strategically... by the net,
The obstacle and barrier,   And the essential component
                            to overcome and...override.

The net,   Not to get caught in,
The net,   Not to get drawn into...

Your opponent's matrix

The Zone...   Is all-encompassing,
It hosts the game...   That is there...
To be won.

To master and transcend.   To go beyond,
Not to falter...   No hesitation,
Just,   Belief!

Nothing else,   Nothing else,
Nothing outside the   Nothing but the game,
    field of vision!

Clarity,
Precision.

Your opponent;
Their will,
Their actions,
Their strengths,
Every shot,
Of the ball.

Until in all...

You know their every
     move,
And...

Dance with no fear,
Grace...

Your movements flow,
The acuity of
     a martial artist,

Your mind becomes
     the sensor,
Attuned to every,
And reflective,

Every adjustment,
Executed.
You are invincible,
Out there.

Synchronicity,

Their mind,
Their body,

Then their weaknesses,
Every bounce,

There is only fusion.

Anticipate...

Obliterate.

All is power.
And deliberation.

Like perceptions...of a Zen Master,
The agility of a dancer.

With radar sensitivity,

Subtle,
Moment.

Micro-calibrated, and...

There is no,

No-one can subdue,   Overcome,
Vanquish.

You are supreme,
And in the supremacy,

There is no,   Out there,

Just a…
Humility.

Yet you are,   On fire,
Your blood carries,   Everything you
Need.

Your cells vitalised,   To respond,
Attack,   Defend…
It makes no difference.

You are,
At
One.

And in the openness,   There is…
Only the zone…

Of
Completeness,
And
Victory.

November 2014

15 The Pulsating Paradox of Parallel 'Cloud Atlas', Worlds

Dreamily, the world outside shimmers…streams on by.
A constant flow, a fluctuating life of flux…Outside the TV
    box.

Gazing out from the refuge of my familiar café,
The lens of my eyes photographs in unfiltered fragments,
The frenzied, and the sleepwalking, a percolating interface,
The myriad palette of the human race.

Expansive and convergent; lost and curious, oblivious and…
Ambitiously jaundiced, deranged, and luminous,
Caught in the fire of Prometheus.
All juxtaposed, simmering to boiling in the cauldron of life's
    heat…
Glazed and…ablaze.

Out of body sensations, floating in between the
Paradoxical spaces of parallel worlds.
A simultaneous co-existence, an outer and inner syncopation,
As I hear the chirping birdsong-twitter,
Voices near, and far, here reposed upon a sequested sofa dais.
A cinematic, panorama glimmers and flickers in no time
    dreamscapes…
In a dissolving, deconstructed conglomeration of unboundaried
    parameters,
A vast microcosmic reconstruction, captured on the retinas…
Glimpses.

An incessantly mutating journey, into an unsequenced theatre,
Interwoven and metamorphosising into a stream of;
Incoherent fragments of reality, and the multitudinous voices of
the inner orator,
Speaking in multi-lingual tongues, a chorus of unorchestrated
vocalists,
All creating disparate sounds in synchrony.
Resonating in a vibrational homogeneity, until all becomes a
film of life embraced,
In a collective consciousness that breathes in the fullness of a
vivacious void.
And at any moment, the reality can capsize, evaporate…transpire.
Wander into the other…another stratosphere,
In a multiverse of transformation and transmigration!

Paper, stone, scissors…replica…simulacra!

All illusions in the mind's television, and world of worlds,
And the plethora of dimensions.

In this evolutionary revolution of reproduction and revelation,
Nothing is as it seems, seamless and suspended…
In the reality of dreaming, replicating life's mysteries,
And exchanging micro-second histories…
Roaming freely on many astral planes.
Above and beyond,
In a *Cloud Atlas*…realm,
Within a consciousness that is beyond reason…

To explain!

July–August 2014

Parallel Universe 60 x 60cm

16 International Women's Day Awakening

The warrior man in me, must rise up to the goddess woman in you,
And the woman in all women.
To become the man that steps out of his juvenile snakeskin,
Knowing that the time is only ever now…to begin.
Not to hide behind the mask of the cowardly unbrave.
Not to continue the masquerade,
Or disguise the feelings gentle inside,
Or waste these awakened gifts by the wayside,
Or hide behind abysmal macho bravado,
That only serves the adulterous myth of the superman.
The illusion…the perpetuated illusion…of, all-conquering man,
Like believing, happiness can be bought in a guru-can.

Deception, an obscured perception…that disguises the demise
    of our deep spirit,
Awakening…and floundering.
To know that the fight is but a fiction of the opposition in you…
The opposition in you.
Seeking outer conflicts, when our hearts are in pain,
And love is someone else's fantasy feeling game.
And don't maim the beautiful and strong, with the
Inner knowing of what's more right…than wrong.
Hiding behind the shirt-tails of: religious bigotry,
Political expediency, fascistic tendency and
Violatory…institutionalised…impotency…impotency!!
Or create subterfuges to justify your ignorance…ignorance!
In order not to rise to the soul's sickness,
Or cower behind the mask of fear, poverty…and wealth,
Or hide in the cemetery of your ubiquitous beliefs,

Or decorate yourself in prejudice...and pseudo-sacrificial...
    wreaths?

The warrior stands brave; not in his nurtured animosity,
Or his ego masturbatory, prancing and posturing,
Or his war-mongering idiocy and impotency.
His strength must manifest...in his resolute...tenderness,
His stance unwaveringly upright, and...agile.

The warrior feels for your freedom...undressed to be expressed,
Unrepressed, and cherished, in each and...every caress,
To bleed with your creed each moon cycle, nurturing the DNA
    in you...
The essence of the I-ching...
In you.

Liberation, emancipation is not to feel with hate,
Not to lose yourself in self-reduced fate,
Bereft, dislocated in an endless...isolating serendipity,
Cloaked in a widow's longing, and reflected...enmity;
Harbouring a deep shadowed ancestral yearning...to heal...
To heal the wounds that have separated us,
To heal the scars, that remind us of the schism,
That has become a spiked defence,
That keeps us on the other side in...escapism.

An open heart illuminates, creates the pathways,
The conduit that leads us in innocence.
Our inner-sense, the beacon, the lighthouse,
That unites us in loving communion and...forgiveness.

March–May 2015

Yoni-moon 60 x 60cm

17 Mannequin Mimicry

Posing in designer labelled rag-trade factory, 'gear and garb'.
Smiling inanely, with constipated, anaesthetised pouts;
Sassafras eyes, sky bright and mesmerising.
Statuesque idols, faceless icons of the fashionados glossed and
    lost.
Manufactured, production-line figurines, crazily…serene.
In products, clothes line identikits, high street composites.
A surreal scenario, each frozen gesture, perfectly feigned,
Designed to encapture,
To feed your cash and carry, impulse, fashion…passion.
Shop-frontage designed, promoting desires and, 'I belong'
    attires.
A two-way bizarre mirror, looking out, looking in.
Identities drowning in replicant, humdrum…bespoke
    in-divisible-banality!
Everyone, just like: well just like, that person over here…and
    just like…that person over there.
An assembly of duplicates…*mannequin mimicry.*
Cat walking the high streets, out or in, out…or…in.
Conveyor belts, self-assembly line out-fitt-ing,
All looking like players in the same fashion game,
Clones gazing, insanely, same-ly…same-ly.
Mummies, modelled behind designer-lit window panes.
Designer this, designer that, not for the fat,
Magazine – photo-shop thin, may only step in,
Stick-insects…cling-ing!
Clinging to what's out, and what's in.
Cling-ing to labelling…fame-show shopping and fashion pill
    popping.

Products on a pop-culture production line charade,
Following in the footsteps on fashion's...yellow-bling
   promo-nade.

January 2015

18 Conversations with Self-Believing

I believe in you, I believe in what you can do!
I believe in you, I believe in what you can do!

You can do, what you need to do!
You can do, what you need to do!

You can be who you need to be!
You can be who you need to be!

Believe in you; believe in me.
We are who we need to be.

We are community in unity,
We are the unity in commune-unity.

We are the breath of life...of life.
We exist, thrive to be...*universe-able.*

Know your beauty has no bounds.
It is infinite and...unquantifiable.

Believe in the purity of your vision,
Believe you can be the transformation...in transition.
Do not dwell in negation,
Believe in the passion of your...mission.
Know you are free...Free in this time...this time.
Believe in you and...
Surrender to your freedom!

The breath of your being, is your surrender to you.
Surrendering in love, is your gift to you.

Know your love will bring you love.
There is only love...this is your gift...to you.

The love in you, is your gift.
There is only love...Feel your gift.

Feel this gift.
Feel this gift.

Give your gift to the universe.
Believe in you...believe your path is...true.

There is no other, there is no other.
Tread your truth...be true to you...your gift is YOU.
Your breath of love...will free YOU.
Believe, believe...believe,

Believe you can be the love that frees you!

Your beauty to be...is the ultimate gift,
You cannot control...the you...in you.

Free the flow, flow freely...from the...
The heart in you.

Your heart-mind...is a feeling-mind.
It feels what you need, it knows...who you are.

Your heart-mind is a free mind...it knows...it knows...
How to love, it knows what love can do.

The beauty of your heart-mind is feeling.
Believe in this feeling, this is your deep self…healing.

The self is the light, light being,
Believe in this light being, the love of your light.

Know your heart-pulse, pulses with all life,
Know your heart-beat, beats with all beings.

Surrender to the love in you…And there is no other.
The love in you, is the light that illuminates…All.

This is your gift, this gift is bountiful and boundless.
It is free…give freely.
Free the love in you.

July–September 2013 and September 2015

19 Electricity

Her kiss made my heart flutter…
The kiss of a stranger…
Out of nothing became everything…impermanent and sonorous.

An open smile, beguiling, an entranced glance…romancing.
Bodies clung undeciphered and unwaveringly, dancing.
An embrace that magnetised…and reversed the tides.
And there was no yesterday or beyond…into a…tomorrow.

Her kiss made my heart flutter, with a honey-bee-frequency.
An irrepressible charge, generating…electricity…e-lec-tri-city,
That opened wide, hearts uncensored…with nowhere…to hide.

Our lips came to rest…kisses unblemished…that,
Became the rain of snowflakes, and sunbeams…fragile,
Evanescently sublime…unsolicitedly…fertile.

An oblique aphrodisiac, abandoned in no time…
That remained suspended between lips…between lips,
Held in our interlaced…fingertips;

Between beating humming-bird wings,
A storm is brewing on the horizon…

Between beating breasts…

Turmoil…and…exhilarated exile.

December 2014 and January–May 2015

Exuberance 121 x 91cm

20 Tabula Rasa

Sufi swirls…silent revolutions,
Round and round, into illuminations and salutary revelations.
Dancing with inner vertigo, let go, let go into incognito.
Uno momento, do you speak the lingo, Esperanto?
Oblivion, obscuranti, beware the vigilante.
Between the eyes of Michelangelo,
Slaves to dancers set in stone, alone…alone,
Stretching out, sinews tensing, grasping into space and time,
And timeless abandon, surrendered…surrendered and…freed.

Whirling, twirling, spinning tops and pointy hats,
Starry eyes all seeing, and infinity gazing,
Roundabout, round-a-bout, round and about, and…out.
Chanting, sounds reverberating, deep, deep down…resounding.
Freed into freedom; each anti-clockwork turn, turning,
Each breath connecting atoms within a universe.

We dance, we dance…
Out of stone we twist and turn,
Citing poems of Hafiz, Rumi, Khayyam and the Rubaiyat,
Soulful expressions of release, infinite, and eternal stanzas,
Quatrains: devotional, absolutional, and revolutional.

Dance, dance into the quintessential realm of…be-ing.
Free ourselves, free yourselves, into no-self-selves.
Orbitary, oscillatory…transformatory,
Uniting the dark and light, into vortical fusion,
Chiaroscuro dreaming, in between worlds of delusion.
Obscuro, obscuro, obscuro.

Sleep into wakeful sonambulance?
Circles of transcendental emptiness and fullness,
A harmonious, balletic dance dialectic,
A joyful ascension into a blissful dimension,
A moving of hearts into stillness and transmission,
A soulful, meteoric, internal transfusion...and astral fission.

Round and round, around pivotal and radius,
Circumference and circumnavigational – inspire-ational,
Devotional, evocational, round and round,
Mystic, mesmeric, rotationally meditational.
Passages of rites, rituals and celestial ceremonies...
Hiatus, epiphany, a divine cornucopian...utopia dwell.
Atom heart, and supreme oneness of be-ing.

A pulsing palingenesis, a spiralling girostasis, around the heart's
    axis:
Radiates, undulates and palpably...pulsates.

Opti-mystic, metamorphic, atavistically cosmic.

Spinning, deeper, deeper into ecstatic stasis,

Soul nature, origin and source.

Dance, Dervish Dance,
Dance the dervish in all of us.
Dance Dervish Dance.

September 2013

21 Spontaneous Combustion

No-one called the fire brigade.
Nor the police...or the ambulance...service.

The ocean is on fire,
A sea of flames.

White waves, moon bright, phosphorescence,
Wave after effervescent wave.

Everything is on fire, its roar and rage,
Consuming our bodies into no-mind...onto a no-self...page.

The fire consumes everything,
Everything is burning with a passion, that rapturously sings.
And love springs, and there is no other music.
The music of fire...the ultimate symphony.

The cosmic ocean is bathed in tantric oneness.
Burning in one flaming inferno,
Its flames engulfing all...in the white heat of erotic...rapture.

An ecstatic immersion within the expansiveness of...
Love and...Sex...

And the orgasmic charge of white...light...bliss.

November–December 2014

22 Doodling: Artlessness to Art Intimacy

A catharsis, an unconscious purgation.

An unravelling of inside-out.

Doodling, 'a dog on a string' stuttering…spluttering, and
strutting.

Expressed gestural secretions,

Streaming from the depths and shallows,

Straight out of an irrational…frying pan.

The pen gliding, hiccupping across open territories.

Creating something.

A something representing,

A something – an…otherness.

An ad-hoc crystallisation, metamorphosising, transmuting,

As it emerges randomly into construction.

A spillage, seeping across a paper ground arena.

Its pathways, linear and curvaceous,

Circumnavigational meanderings; orientating seductively into…

Decorative, figurative and amorphous annotations into some
form of…

Concreteness, illusion…actuality.

The surface indelibly pock-marked; an abrasion, defilement…
revelation,

A plundered metaphor, dredged up archetype,

An unearthed symbolism, a resonating vibration,

In forgotten tongues, dream songs, non-verbalised utterances,

Therapeutic echoes, arising in the silence of distraction.

Doodles forming the: fantastical, diabolic, and somnam-
bulistic.

Nebulous visions of the intangible, illusive and…luminatory.

Marks, coagulating bacteria-like, proliferating into being.
Vacuous, illustrational, reverential, and self-generational.
Organically calligraphic and emblematically...idiosyncratic.

Visual poetry: primal, ancestral, conceptual, prosaic and
    apocryphal.
The doodle breathes, breeds, allows, seduces, mesmerises,
    tantalises,
Agitates and tranquilises.
The simple and the complex, freed from the matrix,
Freed from the matrix.

Acrobatic, prophetic, undeciphered transcripts, disconnected
    inscriptions...Unscripted,
And spiralling in a centrifugal eddying,
Into dispersal, and replicated...dislocation.
And in a moment's absent-mind-fullness...
The pen ceases to scratch, and scar the surface screen...to feel!

All has become: a stroll at dusk, a dance at dawn,
A meander in a flowering meadow,
Twinkling stars in the eyes of storms,
Faces peering out of serpents' mouths,
Vegetable genitals, buttocks on saucers, breasts on plates,
Planets in houses and plants in the anuses of...mouses!
Mice trapped in numberless dice, thrown randomly,
Into a field of mutant rice...sprouting 6D pineal poppy seeds
    for dreaming...
Something nice...Nice!

Just lines, blotches, smudges, and dots dashing into vodka shots.
And Venus seeking Mars and defecating cars.
Sweets dripping rain and the donkey is farting chips again...☺

And roses rise from chimney pots, and eyes are thorns in the
     bots of tots.
And zebra stripes cross the hearts of polka dots.
And all is a stain on the windowpane, as the world inside…
Externalises into a weird and wonderland fantasia…
Lost in play, in astral…A-si-a.

All is in a state of procreation, with bizarre copulations and
     hybrid formulations,
All simmering in a feverish, primeval soup.

Birthing into itness, and suchness; a constant begetting,
And gestating into everything, and…
Nothing…and nothing…is something,
And that something…can be the doodle…
Of everything, we do not know…
In cognition!

August 2015

23 In Search of Something that Eludes All Definition

The perfume permeated all corners, all crevices, all nooks and
   crannies,
All space, defined by fragrance of an undefined particularity.

I bathed in percolating colours mutating, coalescing; and tasting
   of blackness,
And peppered resplendent in star-filled constellations, all moving
   mesmerizingly,
Devoid of nebulous borders and diffused boundaries.

A crescendo of electrons haloed in light waves,
Creating a pulsating harmony; the consummate fugue...yet
   fugitive...
Floating in an aromatic void, seeking permanence in equilibrium
   and concreteness.

A sweet-sour-bitter liqueur.
Sumptuously abundant, drenches each pulsating taste bud in a...
Wet warm, cold dry...paradoxical pungency.
Memories stirred, spawning sporadic thought spores.
Transient...stirrings, causing minefield manoeuvres into stillness,
Merging into an aromatic, oscillatory dance,
Between lights; in an infinite tempestuous dreaming.

Effervescent concomitant notes, uniting and resonating...
Surrendered to life and...love.
Surrendered, and suspended in-between aeons, and vaporised
   epochs.

A return to innocence, bereft of impurity...
Blemish and blasphemy.
The wisdom of placentric music, seismic poetry,
Gestates in an avalanche of beats from hearts...
'Caught in the headlights' of resurrection and illumination.

Void moments, ceasing to be separated at genesis...or at death.
No inbetweenness here, only an unceasingly expanding breath,
That touches the skin of our souls...
And flows with the blood of consciousness.
An energy, a universal being with no concreteness...no
        tangibility,
No anchor, no skeleton, no scaffold, no junction, no crossroads...
        no archetypes,
No-thing-ness, only the fullness of empty-ness...

Only the temporal embrace of space...an eternal hum of womb
        fluidity,
A suspension in love and enveloping life.

Released from the umbilical, liberated from dependency into a
        free, floating existence...fecundity...
Wafting through the ages unchartered, a micro-enormity of
        perpetuating realities...persist...
Know that the tide will flow...equinox and solstice.

There is no choice, but to be part of this capillary current...

Bathed in unknowable fragrances.

March 2014

24 Bristol Sadhu

What is there…but light and love?
Our existence, its purpose, our purpose…our state of being,
Our way to be in this world, on this planet,
Each day giving and receiving love,
Each day, shedding and receiving light,
Each day, being in harmony,
Each day, being in communion,
Each day in non-separate unity,
Each day, smiling with an opened heart,
Each day, hearing the inner music of silence.

Knowing nature, life, my nature is your nature.
Knowing that when you are in alignment…attunement,
The vibration of love and light will adorn you…in bliss,
Will bathe your day in peace and deep tranquillity.

Knowing freedom is always within you,
Knowing freedom is being who you are,
Knowing each beauty-filled breath is an affirmation of life.

And that your path lies within you,
And only you can create this reality.
Knowing that to be…is completeness.
Knowing that to thrive…is to be free from…survival.

Can life be really like this…?
The revolution is within you.

Are you feeling like this…?
Is it really that…

Sadhu seeing simple?

June 2015

25 Viva la Vida

As the skin lies withering on the bone, remember me.
Remember the boy in me; the man in me.
The lover in me, the vital beauty in me.

Remember me as someone who loved life.
Loved to love and loved the gifts of love,

Know I have loved and I was loved, and I knew love,
And love knew me, and there was nothing else to see.

A life of love, a love of life...!

As the skin lies withering on the bone...
And my ashes are scattered to the four winds,
On Zephyr's wings,

Remember me.

VIVA LA VIDA.

May 2014

Acknowledgements

First and foremost, to Kat my lover and companion, for her love, patience and tolerance.

To Dhavyan and Sita my adult children, seeking pathways to peace.

To Pippa, her nimble fingers, mind and smiles.

To Anita, capturing my work from the eyes of her lens.

To Helen, Rowena and Sarah at SilverWood Books, for their enthusiastic engagements.

To the very lovely, encouraging and hospitable staff at Cosy Club on Corn Street, and The Canteen on Stokes Croft.

Ultimately to my parents, their genes and nurture.

Vincent Rymer
January 2016